ANIMALS IN THEIR WORLD

ANIMAL ADAPTATIONS

Patricia Armentrout

A Crabtree Seedlings Book

CRABTREE
Publishing Company
www.crabtreebooks.com

TABLE OF CONTENTS

ADAPTATION

Animals get their looks from their parents. If animals change how and where they live, over a long period of time, their looks and behavior can change for **survival**.

This is **adaptation**.

ANIMALS AND COLOR PATTERNS

Imagine you are a bright green grasshopper. How would you keep yourself safe from hungry birds?

A green grasshopper's best **defense** is being green. Its color works like a pair of **camouflage** pants.

It is harder to find the grasshopper when it is sitting on a green plant.

ADAPTATION INFORMATION

A skunk's black-and-white stripes may warn other animals to stay away—with good reason. Another skunk defense is stinky spray.

Almost all animals have some form of defense. It may be how they look, or it may be how they act.

How is it possible for a big polar bear to sneak up on a resting seal? A polar bear's fur looks white. It helps it blend in with ice and snow.

Under their fur, polar bears have black skin. The skin's dark color soaks in the warmth of the sunlight. This helps to keep bears warm.

Not all animals blend into their surroundings. Many do their best to stand out. Brightly colored animals can use their looks to attract mates.

Male birds often have more colorful feathers than females.

ANIMALS AND BEHAVIOR PATTERNS

Some animals change the way they act, or behave, to help them survive. An octopus, for example, will change its color to match coral and rock. This helps it hide from **predators** such as sharks.

ADAPTATION INFORMATION

An octopus has another form of defense. It sprays a cloud of ink in the water, and then quickly makes its escape!

In some cases, predators need to hide. They take their **prey** by surprise.

Carpet sharks use camouflage to blend in with rocks, sand, or coral on the ocean floor where they wait for their prey.

Tigers live and hunt alone. You might think their pattern of black stripes would give them away. In fact, their stripes can help them hide.

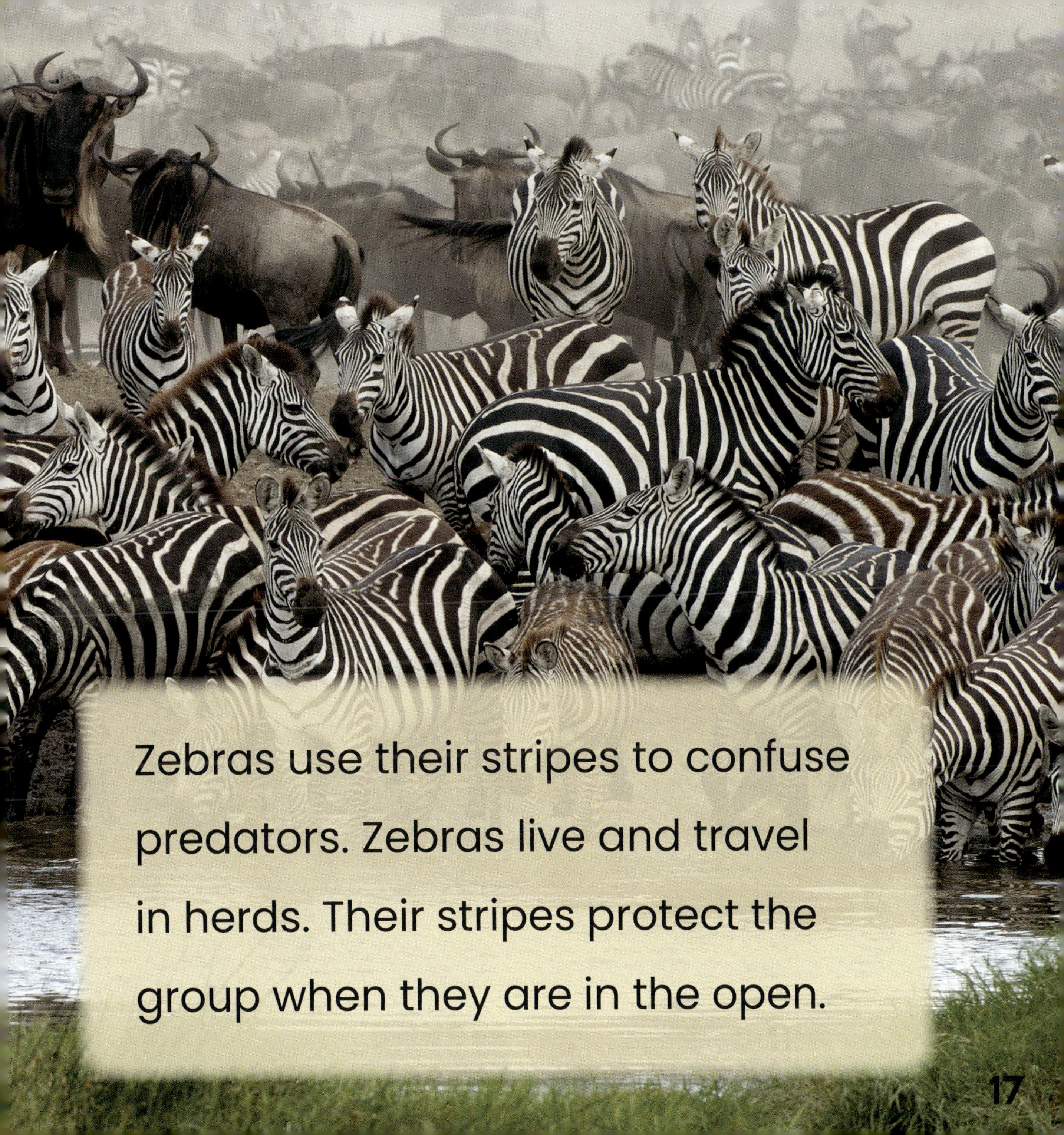

Zebras use their stripes to confuse predators. Zebras live and travel in herds. Their stripes protect the group when they are in the open.

Many animals depend on **instinct** to survive. They are born knowing this behavior pattern.

Adaptation Information

A large school of fish seems to swim and change direction as one. This "safety in numbers" behavior works very well. Predators have a hard time targeting a single fish.

Meerkats must watch out for predators.

Animals such as meerkats rely on family groups to survive. The young learn from the adults.

Why do animals have color and behavior patterns? The patterns are a defense. They give animals the best chance for survival.

Adaptation Information

- Chameleons catch prey with a superlong, lightning-fast tongue.
- Their eyes can look in two different directions at once.
- Scientists believe chameleons change color to send social signals to other chameleons.

Glossary

adaptation (ad-ap-TAY-shun): A process of making changes over a long period of time for survival, including changes in looks and behavior

camouflage (KAM-uh-flahzh): Colors or patterns that blend with the surroundings to help animals stay hidden

defense (duh-FENS): A means of protection

instinct (IN-stinkt): A natural way of acting

predators (PRED-uh-terz): Animals that hunt and eat other animals

prey (PRAY): Animals that are eaten by other animals

survival (sur-VIVE-uhl): The act of surviving, or staying alive

Index

School-to-Home Support for Caregivers and Teachers

This book helps children grow by letting them practice reading. Here are a few guiding questions to help the reader build his or her comprehension skills. Possible answers appear here in red.

Before Reading

- **What do I think this book is about?** I think this book is about how animals adapt to changing conditions. I think this book is about animals in different climates.
- **What do I want to learn about this topic?** I want to learn more about how animals adapt to climate change. I want to learn more about color changes in animals.

During Reading

- **I wonder why...** I wonder why male peacocks have feathers that have colorful eye shapes. I wonder why black stripes on a tiger helps them to hide.
- **What have I learned so far?** I have learned that chameleons have eyes that can look in two different directions at once. I have learned that many animals have natural defense systems to protect them from predators.

After Reading

- **What details did I learn about this topic?** I have learned that many animals hunt and eat other animals for their food. I have learned that octopus spray a cloud of ink in the water to escape from predators.
- **Read the book again and look for the glossary words.** I see the word *camouflage* on page 7, and the word *predators* on page 12. The other glossary words are found on page 23.

Library and Archives Canada Cataloguing in Publication

Available at the Library and Archives Canada

Library of Congress Cataloging-in-Publication Data

Available at the Library of Congress

Crabtree Publishing Company

www.crabtreebooks.com 1–800–387–7650

Print book version produced jointly with Blue Door Education in 2023

Written by: Patricia Armentrout

Print coordinator: Katherine Berti

Printed in the U.S.A./072022/CG20220201

Photo Credits: Cover © Angela Waye; page 23 © Cavan-Images, © page 4-5 © Kris Wiktor; page 6-7 © pattara puttiwong, inset © QiuJu Song; page 8-9 © Volt Collection; page 10 © PASSE; page 11 © Pyty; page 12-13 © Dmitrijs Mihejevs; page 14-15 © Nazir Erwan Amin; page 16 © Andre Anita; page 17 © Eric Isselee; inset page 19 © Frank Gaertner; page 18-19 © Leonardo Gonzalez; page 20-21© Cathy Keifer, page 22 © davemhuntphotography All photos from Shutterstock.com

Published in the United States
Crabtree Publishing
347 Fifth Ave.
Suite 1402-145
New York, NY 10016

Published in Canada
Crabtree Publishing
616 Welland Ave.
St. Catharines, Ontario
L2M 5V6